Angelic Inspirations

by

Theresa Walpole

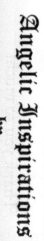

Thank you so much for buying my book.
I sincerely hope you enjoy reading the poems as much as I enjoyed writing them.
I wish you well.

With Love & Blessings

Theresa

Dedication

I dedicate this book to Mr. Leo F. A. Stassen, FRCS(Ed)
MA, FDSRCS, Consultant Oral and Facial Surgeon,
without whom my sister would not be here today.
Also to my pet blackbird of 9 years, Blackie, as he was the
loving inspiration for my first poem. He was my Angel with
black wings.

My "Ode to Leo" and
"Ode to Blackie" are the last two
poems in my book.

First printed and published
November 2004

Photographed, written and
published by Theresa Walpole
E-mail: tesswal@supanet.com
Tel: 01642 814908

Designed and printed by
The Art Room @ CP Offset Ltd.
Kellaw Road
Yarm Road Business Park
Darlington
DL1 4YA

Tel: 01325 462315

An Introduction

The poems in this book are, as the title says, Angelic Inspirations.

I started going to Angel workshops in February 1998 and every day thereafter said Violet Flame Decrees, plus the meditation for Illumination. My creativity was given a tremendous boost. I started doing designs and working with colours and then I took up Calligraphy.

On 27 December 1998, my pet blackbird of 9 years died in my husband's hands. I was extremely upset and felt great sorrow that my dear Blackie would no longer be there each morning with his cheery greeting. A week or so later, from where I didn't know (then), came words in rhyme, my Ode to Blackie. Sixteen months later in April 2000 it was published in my local paper.

Millennium year was THE year for me. I just know I was Angelically inspired as all these wonderful poems came to me. It was a truly magical experience, one I want to share with as many people as possible.

My heartfelt thanks go to my sister Ann, she was my sounding board, to my husband Collin, to my friend Mavis Fielding, Ann Jarvis, Bernard and Simon Lally, Donald Butler and Kev Stevens of CP Offset.

Love & Blessings

Theresa Walpole

Angels of Inspiration

Angels, Angels, help me please, I need your inspiration,
For I know you only come by special invitation.

I am at a loss for words when I do not call you near,
But I know you're close to me and you will always hear,

My loud prayers, my silent prayers, to help me write my lines,
When you are there to help me I recognise the signs,

For thoughts created in my mind are Angelic Inspirations ,
Sent by God through you to me in mindful meditation.

Angels of the Morning

Dear Angels of the Morning, through half closed eyes I peep,
I know you are awakening me from halcyon slumbers deep.

As you brush my sleepy head with Angel wings so bright,
My eyes begin to open, I see your dazzling light,

Resplendent all around you, transmitting beams of love,
On the silver, violet ray direct from Heaven above.

I feel your omnipresence, when each new day is dawning,
Where would I be without you my Dear Angels of the Morning.

Angel Journey

As I sit composing, my mind takes wingless flight,
Soaring upwards ever upwards, on silvery beams of Light.

I can sail uncharted seas and feel the Violet Ray,
Guiding me to crystal shores where Heavenly Angels play,

On golden harps, with golden strings, making music so sublime,
Melodious tunes uplifting me 'til I am lost in time,

And space, that goes beyond the stars, to a splendorous galaxy,
My Angel journey now complete, I am in ecstasy!

Angel Meditation

I light a candle in your name to help me meditate,
I gaze into this golden flame and open swings the gate,

Onto the glittering Angel path where silently I tread,
Into a tranquil world of peace, and before me, just ahead,

A shimmering waterfall cascades into a limpid pool,
I step into this silver lake, reviving, bracing, cool.

I float in crystal waters, relaxing, soothing, calm,
Flowing over me in waves, healing Angel balm.

My Angels linger patiently, then softly call my name,
Returning me on Angel wings to my meditation flame.

Angel Sunshine

Today the sun is shining
After weeks of dismal weather,
I'm sitting in my garden
And I see an Angel feather,

White and softly curling,
Flutter down beside my chair,
I know I m in good company,
My Guardian Angel's there.

From God he's come to tell me,
We should never mind the rain,
For He is there to make the sun
Shine down on us again.

Angel Night

I climb the velvet steps to dreamland,
To God's heavenly domain,
As I float through Angel portals
I can feel the crystal rain,

Falling softly on my forehead,
Like sparkling drops of morning dew,
Mingling with the grace of Angels,
My mind and body they imbue,

With a shower of Cosmic healing,
Bathing me in streams of Light,
Shimmering like the stars in Heaven,
I'm in my perfect Angel night.

I believe in Angels

I believe in Angels, Light Beings from above,
Bringing down God's golden gift of unrequited love.

I believe in Angels, God's messengers of Hope,
Of Joy and Peace and Guidance, each day they help me cope.

I believe in Angels, they guide me through each day,
Always there to help me if I should go astray.

I believe in Angels, they fill my life with joy,
Hovering ever near me, they never would annoy.

I believe in Angels, they help to heal my life,
With caring wings they shelter me and help to banish strife.

I believe in Angels, they surround me like a veil
Of warmth and pure protection, with them I cannot fail.

Yes, I believe in Angels, they bring me utter bliss,
And when I close my eyes at night, they plant an Angel kiss,

On my brow, then I can dream, and float into the Light,
In the knowledge I am safe, within my Angel's sight.

To My Guardian Angel

I am listening for you Angel, but I cannot hear your voice,
If I could hear just one word I truly would rejoice,
To know that you are in the realms of Heavenly Light and Love,
Awaiting me, an earthly soul, to contact God above.

Speak to me, dear Angel, and guide me on my way,
Spur me on to greater things, to the glorious day,
When I will reach my sacred goal, and my heart is filled with peace,
And Love and Light and Laughter and Joys will never cease.

Your message to me Angel, descends into my mind,
'Just remember, dear one, you always should be kind
To others who have hurt you, and one day you will find,
Forgiveness heals a broken heart and a troubled mind".

Angels of Love

Angels of Love spread wide your wings, enfold me in your ray
Of sunshine bright, brilliant light on this dark world today.

I can feel you near me, your warmth upon my arm,
Uplifting and protecting me from any kind of harm.

Please hold this world in your embrace and let your peace abound,
For nowhere on this ailing earth can such tender love be found.

Please assist us all to see the error of our ways,
As we wander round in circles in a never-ending maze.

Direct your love on laser beams, until our hearts they fill,
With wonder, love and perfect peace that lasts till time stands still.

Seeing Angels

Have you ever seen an Angel, just beyond your sight?,
Seen from the corner of your eye in a flash of brilliant light.

In a fraction of a second, it appears, and then it's gone,
Leaving you to wonder if you did gaze upon,

An Angel, in a flash of blue, diaphanous and sheer,
If you behold one you will know your Angel did appear!

Silent Reverie

In deep recesses of my mind,
I find a hallowed place,
Where I can be in touch with God,
My especial sacred space.

I am still, I know my God
Is waiting there for me,
To enter and commune with Him,
In silent reverie.

Angel Smiles

Please , let a smile dance on your lips, and let your mouth unfurl,
There are too many serious people in this despondent world.

A smile comes really from your heart, and deep within your eyes,
Watch out! for there are those that make their smile a good disguise,

To hide behind their feelings, they don't want you to know,
What they re really thinking, so on through life they go,

Feeling miserable and down, they don't know their salvation,
Is just a fleeting thought away, Angelic stimulation!

For when we send our purest thoughts across the Great Divide,
Angels suddenly appear, hovering by our side,

To let their Heavenly beams of love invade our distraught mind,
With wisdom and compassion and remove the chains that bind

Our lips, that have an airtight seal to keep our mouths shut tight,
But Angel smiles can open them and propel us to the Light.

So let these beams pierce your heart, and abandon your disguise,
You'll smile not only from your lips but from your "Angel eyes"!

Space Angel

I'm aboard my Angel spacecraft, ready to take flight,
On a Heavenly journey into the Cosmic night.

I take off in my shuttle at a most alarming speed,
I have no cause to worry, my Angel's in the lead,

In this my Heavenly rocket, hurtling me through space,
With my Angel astronaut at a meteoric pace.

Zooming past the planets, to somewhere far beyond
My imagination, to the healing, golden pond,

Of the one true God source, pool of the Divine,
Where Heavenly drops of nectar fall in streams of jewelled wine.

Good Vibrations

If you wish good health to find,
For your body, soul and mind,
Angels tell us we should be
Vibrating in pure harmony,

With God's Almighty Universe,
Our troubles then will all disperse.

So, think "Angels", meditate,
Tune in, and feel your soul vibrate
With all God's Cosmic Constellations,
Solar streams of "Good Vibrations".

Angel Whispers

I sit in quiet solitude and patiently await,
Angel whispers in my ear, words I can relate,

To those of you who do require a helping hand to find,
Your own dear Guardian Angels who are standing just behind,

Waiting ever patient, to answer your request,
Sit silently and talk to them and they at your behest,

Will do whatever in their power is possible to do,
That fits into God's earthly plan especially for you.

They only offer guidance, you must make the choice,
Be still, listen, you will hear your Angel's whispering voice.

Angel Sleep

Before I close my eyes to sleep, I raise my vibrations,
For I know deep peace will come through mindful meditation.

I visualize, sapphire skies, and shimmering stars of Light,
Encircling me as I gaze into the velvet night.

I know my Guardian Angels, with mighty wings unfurled,
Are reaching out to usher me into another world.

The realms of Light are calling me to take my Angel's hand,
And join them on a journey into a tranquil land.

A place so exquisite and pure, that I would love to stay,
But I must retrace my steps to face another day.

And when from sweet dreams I awake, I am refreshed and cooled,
By streams of Living water, from the Healing Pool.

Archangel Jophiel

I know I truly am inspired by the Angel of Inspiration,
Jophiel, my Heavenly source I meet in contemplation.

I do grounding meditation to call my Angel in,
My thoughts then start to form and flow, now I'm ready to begin.

Words that drop onto my page, fall from Cosmic space,
Forming patterns, oh so intricate of spiritual lace.

You too can reach your Angels, all you need is peace,
Just sit in quiet reverie, your God power you'll release.

Practice makes just perfect and eventually you'll find,
Your Angels will make contact in the corners of your mind.

My words they only come from source on rainbow wings so bright,
Invoked by the blazing Violet Flame of incandescent Light.

Barefoot Angels

There are no dark shadows in my dreams,
Where barefoot Angels tread,
When each night in sweet repose
I lay my sleepy head,

Upon my pillow soft and warm,
I sense my Angels near,
They carry me on drifts of Light
Into an atmosphere,

Of dazzling crystals, drifting clouds,
They gently take my hand,
On a journey purely mystical,
To my "Angelic Wonderland",

Where many, many Angels,
'Midst stars that glint and gleam,
Are dancing barefoot in the Light,
There are no dark shadows in my dreams.

Finding God

Where is God, where do we look to find our dearest friend?,
Is He in rolling thunder, or at the rainbow's end?

He's in each and every flower, in every scented bloom,
In a candle's flickering flame that lights a darkened room.

He's in the softly drifting snow, the mighty roaring seas,
In autumn leaves that rustle in the gently murmuring breeze.

He's in the tiger's powerful pounce, the seagull's haunting cry,
He's in the eagle's soaring wing, the fragile butterfly.

He's also in the shining sun, in moonlight's silvery beams,
In the shifting sands of time and gurgling mountain streams.

He's in the twinkling distant stars, He is everywhere,
God "just is" in everything, He's in our thoughts, our prayers.

He knows what we are thinking, because He's right inside,
Each and every living cell, there's nothing we can hide.

Find God and have a talk with Him, have a two-way conversation,
Meet with Him in solitude for your Heavenly meditation.

Angel Rain

I'm surrounded by green trees and flowers I tend with loving care,
Springing up into the light from Mother Earth so bare.

I water them and feed them, as I know I must,
Then Mother Nature's pixies, sprinkle Angel dust,

Onto every leaf and flower that raises up its head,
It is a shower of Angel rain, God knows they must be fed

By His Almighty powerful hand until the blossoms fade,
They slumber then 'til Spring returns when they are gently bade,

To re-appear and brighten up my garden once again,
And await another shower of Angel pixie rain.

Walking with Angels

Angels please! come walk with me on this God's planet Earth,
Lead me on the spiral path to my moment of re-birth,
Where I will cross the great Divide into a place serene,
More radiant and more beautiful than I have ever seen.

Where I will float on scented clouds and feel peace so sublime,
Surrounded by white Angel wings, transfixed in Cosmic time,
Where choirs of Heavenly Angels sing soothing songs of calm,
Melodious tunes uplifting me into celestial balm.

The Seven Archangels

Each day I find some quiet time to say a special prayer,
And ask the Seven Archangels to keep me in their care.

I ask Michael for protection, Lord Gabriel to guide,
Lord Raphael to heal me and keep me by his side.

To bring great joy into my life, I call Lord Zadkiel,
For pure love to surround me, I pray to Chamuel.

When perfect peace I do require I call Lord Uriel,
And my source of inspiration is of course, Lord Jophiel.

My Angels gather round me as I repeat my invocations,
From God in his omniscience they channel good vibrations.

Inspired with utter joy and peace by the Lords of Love and Light,
I am guarded, guided, healed and loved, forever in God's sight.

Angel Connection

Are you on the Angel wavelength? God's instant link to Source,
Tuning in to Heaven, connecting you, of course,

Via the Angel satellite, the line distinct and clear,
Transmitting earthly messages into the stratosphere,

Where Heavenly messengers await your urgent supplications,
With wisdom they reciprocate on high frequency vibrations.

So if upon this earth you wish to flourish and to shine,
Log on to God's computer, click on the "Angel Line"!

The Road to God

Come, dear friends, take a walk with me
Down the road that leads to God,
All you need to bring with you
Is your Heavenly fishing rod,

So you can catch the pearly beams
Of opalescent Light,
Entrap them and enfold them
'Neath your luminous cloak of white,

Given to you by Angels,
To protect you as you tread,
Upon the rough, uneven path,
Before you which is spread,

Like a map that has no contours,
To direct you to your goal,
For you must find the secret path
To illuminate your soul.

Angel Train

Welcome aboard my Galactic train,
And forward with me go,
On this the Angel Line to Heaven,
Your luggage all in tow.

We will be transported,
By powerful Beings of Might,
Gliding through celestial halls
Of shimmering crystal light.

We'll reach our Heavenly station,
Then we can all descend
Onto the platform that will lead
To our journey's end.

Angelic guides will take us
Where whispering breezes blow,
And soothing Angel voices fall
Like drifting flakes of snow.

Violet Flame Angels

O Angels of the violet Flame I embrace the day we met,
At an Angel workshop where you caught me in your net,

Spun with a million purple strands of gossamer so fine,
You wrapped them all around my heart and also did entwine

Your love and inspiration, for me to find the road
Of spiritual fulfilment, and learn the Angel code,

To help me find my higher self with Angel Flame decrees,
As I repeat them daily, my God power I release.

At first my life remained the same but slowly it did change,
I am filled with inspiration, my life is re-arranged,

I have found my true vocation writing verses in God's name
Through my constant invocations of the "Blazing Violet Flame".

Sacred Space

I am taking you now on a journey,
To a tranquil land of my dreams,
'Tis the Island of Rejuvenation,
Surrounded by radiant beams,

Of Light in its highest vibration,
To heal you with Angelic rays,
This space so special and sacred,
Is yours if you follow your gaze

Into the realms of the Angels,
And cross o'er the Great Divide,
Onto a bridge of Light to find
Your Heavenly Angel guide,

Who greets you in the centre,
And lovingly proceeds
To escort you on this journey,
Supplying all your needs,

For spiritual regeneration,
Immersed in diamond streams,
Of powerful, soulful healing,
On this beauteous Island of Dreams.

Blessings

Has anyone ever upset you, made you feel resentful and cross?
You keep remembering the moment, can't lift yourself out of the dross.

These thoughts keep burning inside you, can't get them out of your head,
There each night before sleeping, still there when you get out of bed.

Why can't you get rid of these feelings, of anger, self-pity and woe?,
The answer to all of your problems, is "just go with the flow",

And bless everyone who's upset you, bless them again and again,
To harbour a grudge is most harmful, it causes you heartache and pain.

Let blessings flow forth from your heartstrings, bless everyone you've upset,
Bless them with love and good fortune, the mould is now being set,

To live your life sending out blessings, to everyone whom you meet,
Whether you've known them a lifetime, or someone you meet on the street.

These blessings will bring inner healing and give you what you're looking for,
Bringing peace to yourself and to others, you've opened your Heavenly Door.

Angel of Dreams

Dear Angel as I go to sleep
Please spin your web of dreams,
Into a shimmering network
Of silver-threaded seams.

Enfold me in your fine spun web,
Silken, glistening, white,
Where I can sleep in sweet repose,
Cocooned in Angel light.

Floating on pure silver clouds,
In rapture sweet I'll lie,
Protected by celestial beings,
'Til dawn breaks in the sky.

Ode to Leo

Mr Stassen, El Supremo,
God's healer here on earth,
You saved my only sister's life,
So to me you're worth

More than a zillion sparkling gems
That bedeck the crowns of kings,
Truly insignificant,
Compared to all the things

You do to benefit mankind,
Priceless is your worth,
King Leo you do reign supreme,
An Angel here on earth!

Ode to Blackie

O Blackie Bird you were my love, and in my garden as I strove,
Did'st follow me from plant to weed, and beside me thou did'st feed
On worms and grubs I had found, as I dug into the ground.

You lived among my shrubs and flowers, sheltering 'neath my plum tree's bowers.
The sweetest song I ever heard, came from you, my dear blackbird,
And as your song rose in the air, you surely took my heart up there.

For nine long years you were my friend, until the day your life did end.
I buried you beneath your tree, where you will be forever free.

I miss you so my lovely bird, for no more will you be heard,
Singing high up in your tree, I truly know that you loved me!